THE TRUTH ABOUT OIL
&
THE LOOMING ENERGY CRISIS

Colin J. Campbell

Produced for ASPO,

the Association for the Study of Peak Oil & Gas,

a network of concerned scientists in universities and

government departments,

now representing most European countries.

First published in 2004

by Eagle Print Ireland

Contents

INTRODUCTION

This booklet offers an insight into this most critical but least understood of subjects. It affects everybody in every country and continent. It needs to be understood if tensions and catastrophes of unparalleled magnitude are to be avoided or ameliorated. It is no good leaving it to politicians – everyone has to understand the essentials in order to plan his or her life and, above all, to give the politicians the mandate for the unpopular actions they will be obliged to take.

These sound like strong words, but don't be deterred by their gravity. Read on and grasp the essentials of our common destiny. The world's economy over the past century has witnessed amazing economic growth, which has allowed the population to expand almost six-fold. It was made possible by a steady, cheap and abundant flow of energy to make the wheels of industry turn, to plough the fields, and provide the fuel for transport and trade. Without it, just about everything slows down – in some cases, eventually grinding to a stop. A city cannot survive without the transport to bring in the food its people need to eat, now commonly coming from distant places. Transport depends on fuel, but oil supply is set to decline.

It follows that there is no easy solution, but find one we must, as we cannot step off the planet. We must learn to cut waste and live differently. The challenges are very great, as the technological lead-times are long and the mental adjustments difficult, affecting the very structure of the societies we know.

But it is not a hopeless cause. We have perhaps twenty years to adapt before oil production need fall below present levels, and even then we face no more than a gentle decline. That said, the transition from growth to decline and the necessary shift in perceptions will be a massive challenge.

At the end of the day, we may find silver-linings in the new world that opens, bringing us into better equilibrium with ourselves, our neighbours and the resources within which Nature has ordained us to live.

OIL DEPLETION: THE HEART OF THE MATTER

The invasions of Iraq and Afghanistan started people thinking about oil. The Middle East and the Caspian are two well-endowed oil regions, contrasting with the United States and Britain, which have both seen their oil production peak and decline. In fact, in the case of the United States, production peaked over thirty years ago, meaning that it has been dependent on rising imports ever since. Britain now reports that its fields will be about exhausted by 2020, making it a net importer within less than five years, on a steeply rising trend. The same pattern is being repeated from country to country. The pressure on imports is set to rise as the list of exporters dwindles and the requirements of countries such as China soars.

The Oil Age commenced about 150 years ago when shallow wells on the shores of the Caspian and in Pennsylvania started to deliver this cheap and convenient form of energy, replacing whale oil as a source of illumination. Production has grown ever since, providing an essential ingredient to modern life – fuelling transport, trade and agriculture. To most people, the regular trip to the filling station seems as much a part of the natural order of things as are the rivers that flow from the mountains to the sea. But whereas the rivers are continually filled by the rains that fall upon the mountains, the oil that supplies the filling station was formed in the geological past and is not being replenished. It is a finite resource which one day will be used up. More importantly, production will soon reach a peak and begin to decline, if it has not already done so.

In earlier years, we had used so little of the resource that the day of reckoning seemed so far away that there was no need to worry about it. We have become so accustomed to its ready availability that we cannot imagine it to be at risk. In fact, we have inherited the mindset of the Industrial Revolution when Man's ingenuity was turned to convert the then near limitless resources of the planet to his benefit. We are conditioned by economic theory to believe that shortage in an open market cannot happen because one resource seamlessly replaces another as the need arises. And we have enormous faith in technology to meet any challenge.

It comes as a shock, therefore, to find that things are not quite what they seemed to be, and that Nature is beginning to tell us that her generosity is not as boundless as we were led to believe. There are limits. The environmental community has been trying to alert us to this for some time, reporting how the wetlands are drying out, how species are becoming extinct, how the climate is changing. These warnings attracted a sympathetic hearing, for no-one wishes to live in a degraded landscape, but they tended to be dismissed as worthy causes rather than something that hit the very heart of our daily lives.

We now face not so much an appeal to protect the beauties of Nature, but the raw necessity of coping with a failing energy supply.

Definitions

> *Economics* is a branch of knowledge concerned with the production, consumption and transfer of wealth;
>
> *Geology* is the science which deals with the physical structure and substance of the Earth, their history and the processes which act on them;
>
> *Politics* are the activities associated with the governance of a country or area, especially the debate or conflict between individuals or parties having, or hoping to achieve, power.
>
> *History* is the study of past events, particularly in human affairs.

The Inquiry Opens

In the preamble, the presiding Judge sets the main terms of reference: in short, to determine the status of oil and gas depletion. He calls as the first witness an historian, so as to cover the importance of the subject and explain how the economic, social and political life of the past century was influenced by an abundant supply of cheap oil-based energy. He explains how petroleum turned the wheels of industry, provided the fuel for transport and trade, formed the raw material for a host of products and, above all, played a critical role in agriculture, fuelling the tractor and furnishing essential synthetic nutrients. He points out how urban populations have proliferated and how they depend largely on oil-powered transport to deliver the food from the countryside, where it is grown. He adds that many already live in abject poverty, so that rising fuel costs would hit them hard.

The Judge observes that the population of the world increased six-fold exactly in parallel with oil production, suggesting a possible link.

He asks the Inquiry to determine whether the economic growth of the past can continue, or whether supply constraints will arise, affecting the very fabric of Man's place on Earth. As he ponders his own question, he resolves to call in bishops and cardinals to address the moral aspects of the matter.

When the Inquiry reconvenes after its initial sitting, the Judge defines the main questions relating to the history of oil and gas discovery. For simplicity, he refers to the various solid, liquid and gaseous phases of petroleum collectively as 'oil', except where there is a need to distinguish them.

He poses some key questions: 'How was it formed and found? Where was it found? What was found? When was it found? How much was found?' He defines the many different categories, from tar-sand to gas-liquids.

More witnesses are called, but each is required to explain his particular bias and vested interest; some are administered a truth serum before they take the witness stand.

The executives of oil companies explain how they have a fiduciary duty to sing to the stockmarket for the benefit of their shareholders, adding that it is simply not their job to explain the nature of depletion. The economists point out that the very foundations of their subject would be at risk if they were to admit to resource constraints beyond the reach of market forces. The exploration geologist admits that his job has degenerated to the point of making purses out of the sows' ears of flawed prospects in the hope of pleasing his employers and earning a livelihood. The politician explains that his voters want only good news, making it easier for him to react to a crisis – which could be depicted as an act of God – than to prepare for one. The investment banker reports that his commissions would suffer if he were to offer anything other than an optimistic view of the future, admitting to no more than short cyclic downturns.

The government official sees his role as encouraging exploration whatever the foreseeable outcome. The even-handed cardinal reminds the Inquiry that Giordano Bruno had been put to death by the Pope on 17 February 1600 for doubting that the Earth was flat, and that Darwin had been accused of blasphemy for proposing evolution in terms of the 'survival of the fittest'.

The Judge decides that the Inquiry will now be structured around three modules:

1. The True Record of the Past

   to establish an accurate record of past oil discovery and production;

2. Forecasting the Future

   to use that information to extrapolate future discovery and production;

3. The Consequences for Manking

   to evaluate the impact on mankind in the widest sense.

1. The True Record of the Past

How was Oil Formed & Found?

Experts speak of sapropel, vitrinite, plate tectonics, global warming, migration paths, anticlines and fault-traps, seals … and many other esoteric technical matters. Men with bronzed faces explain seismic surveys, drilling holes – even horizontal ones – coring, electric logs, semi-submersible rigs and much more. Things called wildcat wells are described. Drillers speak of the 'Kelly bushing' and the 'rat hole', mentioning a pumping well, colourfully termed a 'nodding donkey'. Economists step forward to reveal the tax treatment, whereby operating costs are commonly taken as a charge against taxable income, such that exploration has been largely funded by the unconscious taxpayer. Lawyers speak of concessions and expropriations. A man at the back of the room, with binoculars round his neck, explains that he is an oil scout, charged with collecting information on what is going on in a secretive industry.

But just before the session closes, a distinguish white-haired man in a grey suit rises to his feet, saying that Soviet research has proved that all the theories presented to the Inquiry were erroneous. He claims that oil had in fact originated in the primordial formation of the Earth, such that beneath each oilfield lies another awaiting discovery. An observer from a German geological institute rounds on him, declaring that they had checked the occurrences of oil in crystalline rocks – the basis of the claim – and found that there were perfectly normal explanations in terms of lateral migration from conventional source-rocks.

Many complex scientific and technical matters are covered, some with economic and political attributes and implications.

Where was it Found?

Maps are laid before the Inquiry showing the locations of the world's wildcats (the exploration boreholes that either do, or do not, find new fields), the dry holes (marking the failed attempts), the concession boundaries and the discoveries. The number and size of discoveries are tabulated. The Judge remarks that it is evident that oil is unevenly distributed, noting that clusters of oilfields are separated one from another by vast barren tracts, dotted with dry holes. He further observes that the entire world has been thoroughly explored, pointing out that much of the Southern Hemisphere is rather poorly endowed, evidently for good geological reasons.

What was Found?

Chemists and physicists describe physical properties: the density and viscosity of oil; the bubble and dew points; the nature of asphalt, paraffin and wax. Photographs of free-flowing black oil pouring into a mud pit beside a derrick in the Middle East are compared with those of huge shovels excavating Canada to reach sands impregnated with sticky tar. The mammoth platforms in the stormy North Sea are compared with slender derricks in the desert sands. The energy expended in extracting the many different types of oil is tabulated. One expert reveals his hope of mobilising oil by injecting catalysts into the reservoirs, while another speaks of setting fire to oily shales underground. A Japanese delegate explains how his government had hoped to extract methane from strange disseminated ice-like crystals – called hydrates – in the ocean depths. A representative from the research community speaks of his pressing need for more money, saying that everything could always be studied more.

How Much was Found?

A Texan explains how the Securities and Exchange Commission had moved to prevent fraud by imposing strict definitions in the early days of oil in his state. The ownership of the oilfields, he says, was highly fragmented, such that each owner knew only about his own plot. For financial purposes, he was required to report as *Proved Reserves* only what he expected his current wells or developments to yield. He neither knew nor cared what the fields as a whole might contain. The Judge intervenes to elucidate: 'By *Proved*, you mean in plain language, *Proved-so-Far*, saying nothing about the ultimate size of the field as a whole?'

The Texan nods agreement, adding, 'It's a financial term related to committed investment.' A French statistician speaks with his conviction that it was all a matter of *Probability*, mentioning histograms with *mean*, *mode* and *median* values.

Explorers explain how they made good scientific estimates of the size of a prospect, but had to exaggerate to secure the funds to drill. A Russian recalls the Soviet system of drilling for information without the pretence that every new borehole would make a fortune. Engineers speak of their challenges to balance investment against cash-flow, and of phased developments which aim to accelerate production to payout, followed by satellite and long-reach drilling to extend plateau production for as long as possible. An economist reminds the Inquiry of the impact of discounted cash flow that encourages rapid depletion. An official from Norway tells of the reporting procedures, saying that the explorers' estimates remain confidential, while the expected proceeds of each phase of development are reported as it occurs, giving a comforting image of 'reserve growth'. He reveals that, if pressed, the engineers could report their anticipation of the full future production from a field, no matter what it took to produce the last barrel, but were normally reluctant to do so. He adds that most of the necessary techniques are already well known, so it is simply a matter of judgement to assess how they will be applied. The Judge compliments the Norwegian official on his thorough and open explanation.

When was it Found?

An explorer takes the stand to say that he searched for prospects having the right combination of geological characteristics to contain a viable oilfield. He claims that the date of his recommendation for a successful venture marked the discovery date. A driller counters by saying that the field was found by the first successful borehole. An economist recoils in horror saying that it only became a valid discovery when it delivered a profit, while an engineer says that the first production marked discovery.

The Judge sums up the debate, noting that a field contains what it contains because it had been filled in the geological past. He expresses the view that the most sensible approach is to attribute all the oil ever to be produced from the field to the completion of the first successful borehole, adding with a wry smile, 'You have to be born before you can have a life of any sort.' The bishops and cardinals nod their agreement.

The Judge comments that the different approaches reflect the mindsets and practical circumstances of the different entities involved, and that no deception or conspiracy should be imputed in the diverse responses.

The Clerk of the Inquiry notes the implication of the Judge's findings, namely that all reported reserve revisions are to be backdated to the original discovery, which he feels will have far-reaching implications when it comes to establishing the trends.

The deliberations go on for months as the Inquiry searches for clarity in definitions, transparency in reporting, and cross-examines witnesses to discount their bias. At a certain point, it is decided that the Inquiry should itself travel to gain first-hand knowledge of key oilfields. It wants to understand more precisely the local conditions, conduct technical audits and evaluate the local reporting practices. In particular, it wished to examine the true nature of the huge upward reserve revisions reported by certain OPEC countries in the late 1980s, concluding that they were in part valid, but had to be backdated to the discovery of the fields concerned, which had been found as much as fifty years before.

The Inquiry goes to Venezuela to agonise over where to set the boundary with heavy oil in respect of both past production and reserves. It travels to Canada, finding a different reporting practice because the cold conditions there affect the flow properties of heavy oil, giving the practical need for a higher cut-off.

The Inquiry considers it right to evaluate the degree to which governments are aware of oil depletion and security

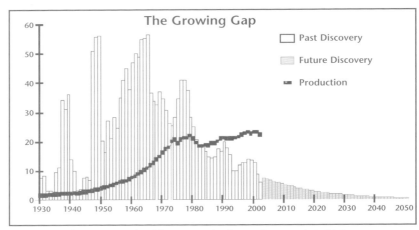

Figure 1: Discovery trends with past production and extrapolated future discovery

of supply, asking to what extent recent events have a hidden oil agenda. It seeks to establish the true nature of the events of 11 September 2001 and their relationship, if any, with control of Caspian and Middle East oil, as well as the Israeli-Arab conflict. In view of the sensitive nature of the subject, it decides to take the evidence *in camera*.

Finally, the Inquiry publishes the first part of its findings in a massive report, giving details of past production and estimated future production from known fields by basin, country and region. Wildcat drilling statistics are included as well. The cover depicts a plot of past discovery, including a simple extrapolation for future discovery, with production superimposed (Figure 1).

2. Forecasting the Future

Armed with comprehensive information on the record of the past, the Inquiry moves on to evaluate various techniques for forecasting future discovery.

Abstract Geological Assessment Couched in Subjective Probability

A representative from the United States Geological Survey (USGS) explains its approach, saying that each geological basin had been identified and delineated in its study. Skilled geologists had pondered the distribution of source-rocks, reservoirs and traps to determine the likely size and number of fields to be found. It was recognised that these were not measurable parameters but expressions of judgement subject to various probability rankings, themselves being subjectively assessed. For example, it concluded that a little-known basin in East Greenland had a 95% probability of containing at least one barrel (described as 'more than zero'), and a 5% probability of containing more than 111.815 Gb (billion barrels), from which a *mean* value of 47.148 Gb had been computed.

The Judge queries if quoting the results of a subjective analysis of a little-known area to three decimal places was justified. The official responds by asserting that the report simply gives the results of 50,000 iterations by a Monte Carlo Simulator, and does not itself express an opinion about how much will be found in the real world, still less forecast production. The Judge returns to the subject saying that it is of extreme importance to recognise that the USGS does not itself forecast future production, but simply reports on a probabilistic model, whose results may be misunderstood by those not versed in probability theory.

The official goes on to explain how the US Geological Survey had assumed that reported growth in *Proved Reserves* in the United States set a pattern for what could be expected in other regions when they had been drilled as intensively. The Judge queries this conclusion, pointing out that the Inquiry had found conflicting evidence showing that the experience of the early days in the United States, with its special commercial environment, was by no means representative of the world as a whole. He directs that only the low end of the USGS range could be taken seriously, noting that actual discovery seven years into the study period has fallen far below the average *mean* value.

An expert from Shell Oil comments that the shape of the probability histogram gives more significant information than any specific number derived from it, adding that the statistical mean value is not necessarily the best estimate of what will be found in the real world. He adds that every prospect is unique – undermining the very concept of statistical probability – while agreeing that it is a useful procedure for comparing prospects, although it does not necessarily give a good indication of what would actually be found.

Creaming Curves

The Inquiry pays particular attention to plots comparing discovery both against wildcat drilling and over time. It notes that many basins demonstrate firm trends of falling discovery, following a hyperbolic trajectory. Countries with more than one basin show more than one such curve. The Inquiry concludes that these plots offer a robust method for forecasting future discovery, accepting the recommendation from an economist that there should be a cut-off before asymptote to exclude prospects too small to be viable under any foreseeable economic circumstance.

Parabolic Fractal

The Inquiry takes evidence from a French expert who explains the distribution of objects in a natural-domain plot as a parabola when size is set against rank on log–log scales. He demonstrates the relationship by showing that the larger towns determine the population of a country as a whole under a fractal law of self-similarity, whereby a complete segment of the distribution describes the whole. Applying the method to oil fields, he notes that the larger fields in any basin tend to be found first and that their distribution can be used to project the total. The difference between the parabolic fractal and what had been found represents the yet-to-find, subject again to an economic cut-off.

Discovery–Production Correlation

The Inquiry notes that discovery in most countries had reached a peak long ago, and that there is a general correlation between the pattern of discovery and the corresponding production after a time-lag. Accepting that oil has to be found before it can be produced, the Inquiry recognises that falling discovery must in due time be reflected in falling production. Accordingly, it determines that the extrapolation of past discovery forms a good basis for forecasting future production. Alternative methods of modelling with a Gaussian bell-curve (also known as a Hubbert curve, after M.K. Hubbert, a distinguished scientist) are also noted.

Other Hydrocarbons

In addition to modelling *Regular Oil* (also known as *Conventional*), efforts are made to forecast production from the following categories:

- Oil from coal and shale
- Bitumen and synthetic oil
- Extra-Heavy Oil
- Heavy Oil (<17.5° API)
- Deepwater oil and gas (>500 m)
- Polar Oil and Gas
- Natural gas liquids from gasfields and gas plants
- Natural gas
- Other gases (coalbed methane, gas from tight reservoirs, hydrates, etc.)

The challenges of doing so are recognised, but the Inquiry does its best, giving emphasis to the engineering and economic factors governing extraction rate, which in most cases are more relevant than the size of the resource itself.

The Inquiry recognises that the depletion of any finite resource has to start from zero on discovery and end at zero on exhaustion, reaching a peak in between. It concludes that peak normally comes close to the midpoint of depletion, when half the total endowment in Nature has been consumed. It also notes that, just as a mountain range appears as a single silhouette on the horizon though actually made up of peaks and inter-montane valleys, the overall peak of oil production may be flanked by valleys and subsidiary peaks.

The Inquiry finds that future production will be influenced not only by physical supply but also by demand – which reflects economic and political circumstances – and especially by the oil price itself. It accordingly contemplates various alternative scenarios. A base-case scenario distinguishes three groups of country:

- Post-midpoint countries – where production declines at the current Depletion Rate (annual production as a percentage of estimated future production);
- Pre-midpoint countries – where production may still rise for a few years, depending on local circumstances. The five main producers of the Middle East (Abu Dhabi, Iran, Iraq, Kuwait and Saudi Arabia, including the Neutral Zone).

On balance, the Inquiry doubts that reported reserves of these Middle East countries can be accepted at face value given the large overnight increases in the late 1980s and the fact that the estimates have barely changed since, despite production. It asks if the reported reserves refer to the amounts found rather than what remains, observing that such a procedure might have made sense from the standpoint of OPEC quota, which was set partly on the basis of reserves, as it avoids the need for perpetual re-negotiation as production changes the relationships.

Taking into account the political situation and other factors, the Inquiry concludes that these Middle East countries are producing at close to their practical capacity, and that their swing role of balancing world supply and demand has all but ended. Accordingly, it envisages that rising demand from economic recoveries will prompt price shocks when capacity limits are breached. The price shocks will, in turn, re-impose recessions, dampening demand and removing pressure on price in a series of increasingly severe vicious circles. The Inquiry foresees a volatile period to around 2010, when world supply will be seen to commence its terminal decline at the then depletion rate of about 2.5% a year. The Judge points out that under this scenario the production of regular oil can be expected to reach an overall peak around 2005, although the volatile situation means that it will not be immediately evident as such.

The Inquiry examines other scenarios, noting that if production could be somehow stepped up, peak would be higher and sooner, giving a steeper subsequent decline. By contrast, an interruption in supply from military action or severe economic recessions would have the opposite effect. The scenarios apply to regular oil only.

The Inquiry recognises that gas will be a partial substitute for oil, but notes that it depletes differently. More has been generated in Nature than was the case for oil, but more also escaped from the reservoirs over geological time because no reservoir seal has perfect integrity. It observes that an uncontrolled well can deplete a gas accumulation very quickly, so in practice gas has been commonly produced below natural capacity to deliver a long plateau, with most fluctuation being seasonal. In effect, production during the plateau period draws down an in-built spare capacity. In an open market, with gas being traded on a daily short-term basis, the end of the plateau comes abruptly without warning market signals, it being cheaper to produce the last cubic foot than the first. The Inquiry speculates that the United States is facing such a collapse now, and that Britain's gas supply from the North Sea is due to fall sharply.

The Inquiry recognises the difficulties of modelling the global supply of gas, because it is so dependent on the con-struction of long-distance pipelines and contractual arrange-ments, which are not easily foreseeable. But it does tenta-tively assume a plateau of production at 130 Tcf/a from 2015 to 2040, followed by steep decline. The production of natural gas liquids is expected to rise and fall in parallel, possibly with some increase in yield from new technology.

The findings of this module are summed up by the graph in Figure 2. As far as regular oil is concerned, the key parameters (in rounded numbers, as of the end of 2003) are as follows:

Past production	920 Gb
Future Production	930 Gb
From known fields: 780 Gb	
From new fields: 150 Gb	
Total	1850 Gb

The Inquiry accepts that the forecast therein projected will be subject to many unpredictable short-term factors. However, it concludes that the departures will not be great, and that the model is a useful basis upon which to assess the general consequences for Mankind (*see* module 3). The Inquiry draws attention, in particular, to a certain self-adjusting feature of the model whereby short-term departures are balanced by higher or lower depletion rates for the remainder.

After months of detailed investigations, taking evidence far and wide, searching for the truth amidst conflicting viewpoints and vested interests, the Inquiry braces itself for its most challenging task. That is to determine what the depletion of oil and gas means for Mankind, and what practical steps may be taken to ameliorate any adverse consequences.

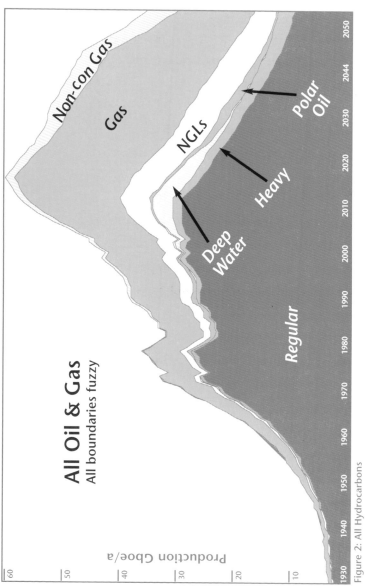

Figure 2: All Hydrocarbons

3. The Consequences for Mankind

The Judge decides to bring in philosophers, moralists, Church leaders, thinkers, leaders and representatives of all walks of life. He recognises that new ground has to be covered that goes beyond conventional mindsets and academic structures. There is room for the intuitive common sense of a farmer from West Cork.

This part of the Inquiry opens with a review of the dependency of the modern world on oil for almost all aspects of life, and moves on to analyse the bedrock of economic theory. This in turn prompts a review of the underlying criteria behind government policy and the democratic process – also called spin. From there, the debate leads to the identification of the attitudes and aspirations of people in their daily lives, touching on issues of morality in its widest sense. In particular, the morality of profiteering is evaluated, recognising that morality and the common good often run in parallel. The cardinals offer their spiritual insights. New-wave economists seek to integrate the hidden environmental costs of industry and trade into the framework of market economics.

It is found helpful to compare modern attitudes and aspirations with those prevailing under different past circumstances, as for example obtained in wartime Britain. Basic needs were then in short supply, and the open market was replaced by a policy of central control, aimed to allocate fair shares of what was available.

Many weeks of fruitful investigation pass before the Judge makes his summing up. He succeeds in synthesising the conclusions into a few key points, which he lists as follows:

1 Peak Production
2 Subsequent Decline
3 Conflict
4 Economic Impact
5 Options

1. Peak Production

The Inquiry finds that world production of regular oil will reach a peak during the first decade of the twenty-first century, and that production of all liquids will likewise peak around the end of the decade. Such a peak reflects the immutable physics of the oil reservoirs and the rate of past discovery, being virtually immune to economic or technological developments. It adds that economic recession dampens demand. Peak is accordingly delayed by any reduction in demand, such that it would have been passed in 2003 should demand move into long-term decline.

2. Subsequent Decline

The Inquiry finds that economic and technological developments may affect the rate of post-peak decline and stimulate the entry of substitutes from so-called renewable
energies, including safe nuclear energy.

3. Conflict

The Inquiry notes that the uneven distribution of future production and demand gives serious grounds for conflict as
consumers vie with each other for access to supply, princi-
pally from the Middle East.

4. Economic Impact

The Inquiry notes that a decline in the supply of cheap oil-
based energy will have an unavoidable and far-reaching
impact on the economic condition of the world, especially
in respect of trade and food supply. It may, on the other
hand, have a positive impact on the environment generally.
For example, climate-change concerns might evaporate
from reduced emissions, and fish-stocks might recover if
trawling gives way to less energy-intensive drift netting.

5. Options

The Inquiry concludes that the world has three main
options in addressing the issue. Two are short-term options

with negative attributes, but in the longer term all three paths come together to reflect the eventual depletion of oil, which is far beyond Man's control, being imposed by Nature (the identified options are graphically illustrated in Figure 3, *below*).

· *Option 1: National Profiteering*
Under this option, oil resources remain within the national jurisdictions of the producing countries, allowing them to profiteer from the scarcity value of their oil as world shortages bite in earnest during the first decade of the twenty-first century. It is feared that such profiteering could lead to

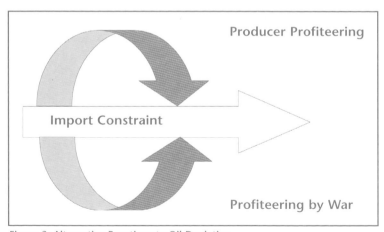

Figure 3: Alternative Reactions to Oil Depletion

excessive military expenditure or reinvestment in overseas industrialised countries, leading to large-scale transfers of ownership, which would be causes of predictable tension. Furthermore, the profiteering will likely prompt world recession that might be detrimental to the profiteer. National profiteers will also suffer in the longer term because they would be less prepared to meet the consequences of the inevitable exhaustion of their natural inheritance.

- *Option 2: Profiteering by War*

Under this option, one or more major consuming countries use their military might to take control of oil production, wherever it might lie, with a view to profiteering from such control, both directly from the sale of conquered oil and indirectly by stimulating their home economies with cheap energy. If world production were stepped up under this arrangement, the global peak would be higher and sooner, meaning that the subsequent decline would be steeper, making a bad situation worse. While this too might convey short-term benefits, it leaves the conquerors less prepared to cope with the inevitable decline imposed by Nature, which would be even steeper as a result of their actions.

- *Option 3: Consumer Restraint*

The third option contemplates a Depletion Protocol

whereby the importers of oil cut their imports to match the global depletion rate, as imposed by Nature, which is currently running at about 2.5% a year. By matching demand with supply, world prices remain in reasonable relationship with production cost, removing profiteering, which is held to be morally wrong. It means that the poor countries will be able to afford their minimal requirements. It also means that the massive destabilising financial transfers arising from option 1 (national profiteering) are avoided. The importing countries can manage their allocations as suits their particular environments and inclinations. They may auction the supply to the highest bidder under open-market principles; they may tax oil higher with corresponding reductions of other taxation; they may ration supplies, such rations being perhaps tradable; or they may employ a combination of such measures.

The Inquiry concludes that this option provides the smoothest transition to the new world of reduced energy supply. It encourages the reduction of waste and stimulates the entry of renewable energies to the maximum extent possible. It further brings many indirect benefits, leading to the encouragement of local communities and markets, which allow people to find themselves in better harmony with themselves, each other and their environments.

THE OIL DEPLETION PROTOCOL

The Inquiry's lawyers formulate an outline draft Depletion Protocol, which becomes a consultative document for consideration by government and political parties alike.

- WHEREAS history has recorded an increasing pace of change, such that the demand for energy has grown rapidly in parallel with the world's population over the past 200 years since the Industrial Revolution;

- WHEREAS the energy supply required by the population has come mainly from coal and petroleum, having been formed but rarely in the geological past, such resources being inevitably subject to depletion;

- WHEREAS oil provides 90% of transport fuel, essential to trade, and plays a critical role in agriculture, needed to feed the expanding population;

   WHEREAS oil is unevenly distributed on the planet for well-understood geological reasons, with much being concentrated in five countries, bordering the Persian Gulf;

- WHEREAS all the major productive provinces of the world have been identified utilising improving technology and advancing geological knowledge, it being now evident that discovery reached a peak in the 1960s;

- WHEREAS the past peak of discovery inevitably leads to a corresponding peak in production during the first decade of the twenty-first century, assuming no radical decline in demand;

- WHEREAS the onset of the decline of this critical resource affects all aspects of modern life, such having grave political and geopolitical implications;

- WHEREAS it is expedient to plan an orderly transition to the new world environment of reduced energy supply, making early provisions to avoid the waste of energy, stimulate the entry of substitute energies, and extend the life of the remaining oil;

- WHEREAS it is desirable to meet the challenges so arising in a co-operative and equitable manner, such to address related climate-change concerns, economic and financial stability and the threats of conflicts for access to critical resources.

Now it is Proposed that:

1. A Convention of nations shall be called to consider the issue with a view to agreeing an Accord with the following objectives:

    -   To avoid profiteering from shortage, such that oil prices may remain in reasonable relationship with production cost;
    -   To allow poor countries to afford their imports;
    -   To avoid destabilising financial flows arising from excessive oil prices;
    -   To encourage consumers to avoid waste;
    -   To stimulate the development of alternative energies.

2. Such an Accord shall have the following outline provisions:

    -   No country shall produce oil at above its current depletion rate, such being defined as annual production as a percentage of the estimated amount left to produce;
    -   Each importing country shall reduce its imports to match the current world depletion rate, deducting any indigenous production.

3. Detailed provisions shall cover the definition of the several categories of oil, exemptions and qualifications, and the scientific procedures for the estimation of depletion rate.

4. The signatory countries shall cooperate in providing information on their reserves, allowing full technical audit, such that the depletion rate may be accurately determined.

5. The signatory countries shall have the right to appeal their assessed depletion rate in the event of changed circumstances.

PLAN OF ACTION

Let us hope that the envisaged Inquiry need not remain hypothetical for much longer. In any event, we now turn to a short list of practical proposals for consideration by everyone. Some steps call for government action arising from local and regional pressures based on the new understandings. The proposals are designed to help individuals adapt their own lives so as to be better prepared. Children in particular need to be informed of the new directions so as to have more realistic aspirations and less disturbing disappointment.

1. Study & Inform

The most urgent need is to undertake a properly funded study of what the actual world oil and gas situation is. Public data are grossly unreliable and misleading, so it is necessary to access industry data, or, better still, use national foreign services to collect the information first hand in a systematic way. The pronouncements of the International Energy Agency, to which many countries belong, can be safely ignored insofar as it sees its role merely as a politically correct consumers' lobby – one that does not conduct proper scientific analysis itself. The European

Union, likewise, is reluctant to grasp the nettle of this very sensitive issue. By not studying the issue itself, it is politically free of the results that such a study would deliver. So, every country and region needs to stand on its own feet, and set up small independent units to make the analysis, which is not particularly difficult, once the essential data are gathered.

The second step is to launch a vigorous programme of public information so that everyone shall understand the essentials. The people need to recognise particularly that depletion is imposed by Nature and that growing shortage and price do not necessarily speak of fraud, conspiracy, gouging and profiteering, although it may well be accompanied by such behaviour. Popular understanding is essential to provide government with the mandate for the actions it has to take.

2. Avoid Waste

When things become short and expensive, the most obvious response is to use less of them. The waste of energy in the modern world is colossal, so there is great scope for more efficient usage. This in turn calls for a national process of energy audit because people, used to past practices, are simply not aware of how wasteful they are. It has been just too easy to flick a switch. Developing expertise in energy audit and management will deliver dividends at little pain. As this process evolves, fiscal incentives and penalties will have to be introduced through utility charges from factory to home. It should become cheaper to own a car but more expensive to use one; 'gas-guzzlers' need to be penalised relative to efficient vehicles. Corporate tax arrangements need to be overhauled so that transport costs are no longer taken as a charge against taxable income. There is no reason for airlines to continue to enjoy tax-free fuel. The free market can be allowed to operate within the overall new provisions, but eventually it may be useful to provide everyone with a certain minimal ration at affordable cost, paid for by penalising excess. The ration itself could be tradable, becoming a form of currency, as some economists suggest.

3. *Renewable Energy*

Minimal progress has been made so far towards renewable energies simply because they do not easily compete with fossil fuels being dumped onto the market at far below replacement cost – that being, in fact, infinitely high. The market principle of discounted cash flow favours the short-term solution chasing the illusion of perpetual growth, but is contrary to the new reality imposed by Nature. Tides and winds can be harnessed. Every south-facing roof can have a solar collector for hot water or electricity. The heat-pump, which is a form of refrigerator in reverse, can pump out four times more heat than the energy it consumes. Hydroelectric projects, including small-scale ones, can be installed wherever possible. Farmers can grow bio-mass on one field to fuel the tractors on another. Although it is emotionally sensitive, there might even be a case for re-examining the nuclear option.

Renewable energy projects are probably best conducted at the local level. Communities should take responsibility for their prime energy supply, while tapping into the national grid to contribute surplus or to supplement their own capacity. The growth of local markets may well carry hidden benefits, bringing a greater sense of shared responsibility in positive communities to which people feel they belong.

The following datasheets give the essential information on the oil-resource base by country, region and the world.

1. *Production of Regular Oil by Country*
2. *Production Forecast*
3. *Regular Oil by Region*
4. *Production Forecast for Other Categories of Oil & Gas*
5. *Production Forecast for Gas & Gas Liquids Gas (at 6Tcf = 1 Gboe)*
6. *Production Forecast for All Oil & Gas*
7. *Balance with 1.5% Annual Demand Growth*

1. Production of Regular Oil by Country

Date 2003	#1	FROM KNOWN FIELDS — Present 2003	Past	Reported Reserves — World Oil	O&GJ	% Reported	Future	NEW FIELDS	TOTAL	PEAK	DATES
See notes below	#1	#2	#3	#4	#5	#6	#7	#8	#9	#10	#11
Unit		kb/d	Gb	Gb	Gb		Gb	Gb	Gb		
Saudi Arabia	A	8430	97.3	259.3	259.4	180%	144.1	18.6	260	1948	2008
Russia	B	8216	127.1	59.8	60.0	100%	60.0	12.9	200	1960	1987
US-48	C	4215	172.1	22.0	22.7	110%	20.6	2.3	195	1930	1971
Iran	A	3730	55.7	100.1	125.8	250%	50.3	14.0	120	1961	1974
Iraq	A	1275	27.9	115.0	115.0	180%	63.9	18.2	110	1928	2021
Kuwait	A	1850	31.5	96.5	96.5	160%	60.3	3.2	95	1938	2014
Venezuela	D	1713	46.8	53.1	77.8	225%	34.6	6.2	88	1959	1970
China	B	3415	29.8	23.7	18.3	75%	24.3	5.8	60	1964	2012
Abu Dhabi	A	1850	18.6	61.9	92.2	250%	36.9	4.5	60	1961	1970
Libya	E	1400	23.4	30.0	36.0	120%	30.0	3.6	57	1967	2006
Nigeria	E	2120	23.2	32.0	25.0	90%	25.0	2.8	51	1997	2003
Mexico	D	3365	31.2	17.2	15.7	100%	17.4	1.4	50	2000	2033
Kazakhstan	B	887	6.3	-	9.0	25%	36.0	7.7	50	1974	1999
UK	F	2095	20.4	4.5	4.7	45%	10.4	1.2	32	1979	2001
Norway	F	3035	17.4	9.0	10.4	90%	11.6	3.0	32	1993	1977
Indonesia	G	1020	20.2	5.9	4.7	50%	9.4	1.4	31	1956	2006
Algeria	E	1050	12.5	13.0	11.3	85%	13.3	2.2	28	1958	1973
Canada	C	1100	19.2	5.5	178.9	3500%	5.1	0.7	25	1951	2005
N.Zone	A	600	6.8	4.7	5.0	100%	5.0	3.2	15	1871	2009
Azerbaijan	B	303	8.2	-	7.0	80%	8.8	3.0	20	1962	2001
Oman	H	822	7.3	5.7	5.5	79%	7.0	0.4	15	1965	1995
Egypt	E	750	8.9	2.4	3.7	102%	3.6	0.2	13	1994	1998
Argentina	D	720	8.5	2.8	2.8	85%	3.3	1.2	12	1940	2000
Qatar	H	720	6.8	15.6	15.2	375%	4.9	1.3	12	2004	1997
India	G	665	5.8	4.6	5.4	110%	4.9	0.4	12	2001	2003
Malaysia	G	800	5.6	4.3	3.0	75%	4.0	0.4	10	1999	1999
Colombia	D	540	5.9	1.6	1.8	50%	3.7	1.6	10	1971	1998
Angola	E	640	4.5	8.9	5.4	140%	3.9	1.6	10	1997	2000
Australia	G	530	6.0	3.7	3.5	135%	2.6	0.7	9.3	1857	1976
Romania	B	116	5.8	1.1	1.0	60%	1.6	0.6	8.0	2007	2004
Ecuador	D	410	3.4	4.6	4.6	125%	3.7	0.9	8.0	1966	1995
Syria	H	528	4.0	2.3	2.5	100%	2.5	0.5	7.0	1995	1986
Brasil	D	494	4.8	9.8	8.5	425%	2.0	1.2	7.0	1964	1973
Turkmenistan	B	200	3.0	-	0.5	30%	1.8	1.2	6.0	1970	1991
Dubai	H	330	3.9	1.1	4.0	325%	1.2	0.2	5.3	1985	1996
Gabon	E	240	2.9	2.4	2.5	170%	1.5	0.1	4.5	1983	1978
Trinidad	D	135	3.2	1.0	1.0	85%	1.2	0.1	4.5	1987	1978
Brunei	G	190	3.1	1.1	1.4	150%	0.9	0.3	4.3	1962	1970
Ukraine	B	83	2.6	-	0.4	40%	1.0	0.4	4.0	1978	1999
Yemen	H	350	1.7	2.9	4.0	300%	1.3	0.4	3.5	1988	1983
Peru	D	87	2.4	1.0	0.3	40%	0.7	0.4	3.5	1971	2002
Denmark	F	368	1.5	1.8	1.3	100%	1.3	0.4	3.3	2008	2005
Vietnam	G	333	1.0	2.5	0.6	30%	2.0	0.2	3.3	1984	2001
Congo	E	240	1.6	1.5	1.5	210%	0.7	0.4	2.8	1952	1966
Germany	F	78	2.0	0.3	0.4	100%	0.4	0.1	2.5	1971	1981
Tunisia	E	66	1.2	0.5	0.3	50%	0.6	0.4	2.2	1992	1998
Uzbekistan	B	150	1.1	0.7	0.6	75%	0.8	0.3	2.0	1981	1997
Italy	F	96	0.9	0.7	0.6	50%	1.1	0.6	2.0	1980	2005
Sudan	E	233	0.3	0.7	0.6	50%	1.1	0.6	2.0	1977	2008
Chad	E	100	0.0	-	-	-	1.2	0.8	2.0	2007	2005
Thailand	G	160	0.5	0.5	0.6	105%	0.6	0.5	1.5	1977	1986
Cameroon	E	66	1.1	-	0.4	140%	0.3	0.3	1.4	2016	2016
Bolivia	D	30	0.4	0.9	0.4	70%	0.6	0.1	1.3	1964	1987
Hungary	B	24	0.7	0.1	0.1	20%	0.5	0.0	1.3	1932	1970
Bahrain	H	32	1.0	-	0.1	60%	0.2	0.2	1.2	1980	1989
Netherlands	F	46	0.8	0.1	0.1	60%	0.2	0.2	1.2	1969	1991
Turkey	H	45	0.8	0.3	0.3	150%	0.2	0.2	1.0	1950	1988
Croatia	B	21	0.5	0.1	0.1	24%	0.3	0.1	1.0	1958	1988
France	F	25	0.7	0.2	0.1	95%	0.2	0.1	0.9	1947	1955
Austria	F	18	0.8	0.1	0.1	60%	0.1	0.0	0.9	2001	1992
Pakistan	G	60	0.5	0.3	0.3	100%	0.3	0.2	0.9	2008	1993
Papua	G	48	0.4	0.4	0.2	80%	0.3	0.2	0.9	1980	1998
Sharjah	H	45	0.5	-	1.5	1000%	0.2	0.1	0.8	1928	1983
Albania	B	6	0.5	0.4	0.2	85%	0.2	0.1	0.8	1979	1982
Chile	D	10	0.4	0.0	0.2	600%	0.0	0.1	0.5	1979	1982
REGIONS											
ME Gulf	A	17735	237.9	637	694	188%	368.9	59.2	666	1948	1974
Eurasia	B	13421	185.8	85	97	71%	136.0	32.3	354	1964	1987
N.America	C	5141	191.2	27	202	784%	25.7	3.1	220	1930	1972
L.America	D	7504	107.1	92	113	168%	67.2	12.7	184	1977	1998
Africa	E	6875	80.0	93	87	107%	81.2	5.3	174	1961	2006
Europe	F	5761	44.5	17	18	71%	25.0	5.1	75	1974	2000
East	G	3806	43.0	92	20	79%	24.9	5.1	73	1967	2000
ME. Other	H	2872	26.2	28	33	199%	16.6	2.6	46	1965	1998
Other		552	3.6	-	0	100%	0.5	5.5	10	1956	2007
Unforeseen	I						35.0	13.4	48		
Non-ME Gulf		45930	681	365	569	138%	412	90	1184	1956	2003
WORLD		63665	919	1003	1263	162%	781	150	1850	1964	2005

Notes
#1 Regional Code ("Unforeseen" is a balancing item to give a rounded total)
#2 2003 Production in thousands of barrels per day (kb/d)
#3 Total paast production in billions of barrels (Gb)
#4 Proved Reserves as reported by World Oil
#5 Proved Reserves as reported by the Oil & Gas Journal
#6 Percentage reported as assessed after removal for non-Regular oil and spurious entries
#7 Estimated future production from known fields to 2075
#8 Estimated future production from new fields to 2075
#9 Estimated total production to 2075
#10 Date of peak discovery
#11 Date of peak production

2. Production Forecast

Mb/d	2000	2005	2010	2020	2050
Russia	6.3	9.1	10.0	4.5	0.7
Saudi Arabia	8.0	8.4	8.4	7.2	3.6
Iran	3.7	3.7	3.4	2.7	1.4
US-48	4.5	3.6	2.6	1.4	0.2
China	3.2	3.1	2.6	1.7	0.5
Mexico	3.0	3.0	2.2	1.1	0.2
Norway	3.2	2.6	1.8	0.9	0.1
Nigeria	2.0	2.3	2.1	1.5	0.5
Iraq	2.6	2.7	2.9	2.9	1.9
Kuwait	1.8	1.9	1.9	1.9	1.3
Abu Dhabi	1.9	1.9	1.9	1.9	0.9
UK	2.5	1.8	1.3	0.7	0.1
Venezuela	2.6	1.7	1.5	1.3	0.8
Libya	1.4	1.5	1.9	1.6	0.7
Kazakhstan	0.7	1.0	1.2	1.8	1.3
Canada	1.1	1.0	0.7	0.4	0.0
Indonesia	1.3	1.0	0.8	0.6	0.2
Canada	1.0	1.3	2.0	a2.8	3.9
Oman	0.9	0.8	0.6	0.4	0.1
Malaysia	0.7	0.7	0.5	0.3	0.0
Azerbaijan	0.3	0.7	0.8	0.6	0.2
Egypt	0.8	0.7	0.5	0.2	0.0
Qatar	0.7	0.6	0.5	0.3	0.1
India	0.6	0.6	0.5	0.4	0.1
Argentina	0.8	0.6	0.4	0.2	0.0
N.Zone	0.6	0.6	0.5	0.4	0.2
Angola	0.7	0.6	0.5	0.3	0.1
Colombia	0.7	0.5	0.4	0.2	0.1
Australia	0.7	0.5	0.4	0.2	0.0
Syria	0.5	0.5	0.3	0.2	0.0
Brasil	0.4	0.4	0.3	0.1	0.0
Ecuador	0.4	0.4	0.4	0.3	0.1
Denmark	0.4	0.3	0.2	0.1	0.0
Yemen	0.4	0.3	0.2	0.1	0.0
Vietnam	0.3	0.3	0.3	0.1	0.0
Dubai	0.3	0.3	0.2	0.1	0.0
Chad	0.0	0.2	0.2	0.1	0.0
Sudan	0.2	0.2	0.2	0.1	0.0
Gabon	0.3	0.2	0.2	0.1	0.0
Congo	0.3	0.2	0.1	0.1	0.0
Turkmenistan	0.1	0.2	0.2	0.1	0.1
Brunei	0.2	0.2	0.1	0.1	0.0
Thailand	0.1	0.2	0.1	0.1	0.0
Uzbekistan	0.2	0.1	0.1	0.1	0.0
Trinidad	0.1	0.1	0.1	0.1	0.0
Romania	0.1	0.1	0.1	0.1	0.0
Italy	0.1	0.1	0.1	0.1	0.0
Peru	0.1	0.1	0.1	0.1	0.0
Ukraine	0.1	0.1	0.1	0.1	0.0
Germany	0.1	0.1	0.1	0.0	0.0
Tunisia	0.1	0.1	0.1	0.0	0.0
Cameroon	0.1	0.1	0.0	0.0	0.0
Pakistan	0.0	0.1	0.0	0.0	0.0
Papua	0.1	0.0	0.0	0.0	0.0
Netherlands	0.0	0.0	0.0	0.0	0.0
Turkey	0.1	0.0	0.0	0.0	0.0
Sharjah	0.1	0.0	0.0	0.0	0.0
Bolivia	0.0	0.0	0.0	0.1	0.0
Bahrain	0.0	0.0	0.0	0.0	0.0
Hungary	0.0	0.0	0.0	0.0	0.50
France	0.0	0.0	0.0	0.0	0.0
Croatia	0.0	0.0	0.0	0.0	0.0
Austria	0.0	0.0	0.0	0.0	0.0
Chile	0.0	0.0	0.0	0.0	0.0
Albania	0.0	0.0	0.0	0.0	0.0

3. Production Forecast for Regular Oil by Region

Regular Oil by Country	2000	2005	2010	2020	2050
ME Gulf	18.5	19.5	19.0	17.0	9.3
Eurasia	11.1	14.4	15.1	9.1	3.0
N.America	5.5	4.5	3.3	1.8	0.3
L.America	8.0	6.8	5.4	3.5	1.3
Africa	6.7	7.4	7.1	5.0	1.8
Europe	6.3	5.0	3.6	1.8	0.3
Far East	4.0	3.5	2.8	1.7	0.4
ME. Other	2.9	2.6	1.9	1.1	0.2
Other	0.5	0.6	0.6	0.4	0.1
Unforeseen		0.0	0.0	0.1	2.2
Non-MEGulf	45	45	40	24	10
MEGulf Share %	29%	30%	32%	41%	50%
WORLD	64	64	59	41	19

Excluding: tar, heavy, deepwater, polar oil & PNGL

4. Production Forecast for Other Categories of Oil & Gas

Oil

	2000	2005	2010	2020	2050
Heavy Oils (1)	1.4	2.6	3.4	4.3	5.7
Canada	1.0	1.3	2.0	2.8	3.9
Venezuela I	0.5	0.5	0.5	0.6	1.1
Venezuela II	0.0	0.7	0.7	0.7	0.2
Other	0.0	0.2	0.2	0.3	0.5
Deepwater (2)	1.3	5.6	8.4	3.8	0.1
G. Mexico	0.7	2.0	2.1	0.9	0.0
Brasil	0.6	1.5	1.8	0.8	0.0
Angola	0.0	0.8	2.2	0.7	0.0
Nigeria	0.0	0.5	1.4	0.4	0.0
Other	0.0	0.8	1.0	1.0	0.1
Polar	1.0	0.9	0.9	2.1	0.4
Alaska	1.0	0.8	0.6	0.4	0.1
Other	0.0	0.1	0.3	1.7	0.3
Other (3)	0.0	0.1	0.3	0.5	1.0
Subtotal	3.7	9.2	13.0	10.7	7.2

5. Production Forecast for Gas & Gas Liquids Gas (at 6Tcf = 1 Gboe)

	2000	2005	2010	2020	2050
Gas	39.2	45.2	52.6	59.5	35.6
Non-con gas	1.4	1.9	2.5	4.1	10.1
Subtotal	40.5	47.1	55.1	63.6	45.8
Gas Liquids					
NGL (4)	6.3	8.2	9.3	10.7	6.3

6. Production Forecast for All Oil & Gas

	2000	2005	2010	2020	2050
Gas	40.5	47.1	55.1	63.6	45.8
Liquids	73.6	81.4	81.3	62.9	32.5
Processing Gain	1.5	1.6	1.6	1.3	0.7
Total	115.7	130.2	138.0	127.7	78.9

7. Balance with 1.5% Annual Demand Growth

(Liquids Mb/d)	2000	2005	2010	2020	2050
Supply	75.1	83.1	82.9	64.1	33.2
Demand	75.0	80.8	87.0	101.0	158.0
Balance	0.0	2.3	-4.1	-36.9	-124.8

Notes

Regular Oil includes condensate (in oilfields).
(1) Bitumen, Extra-Heavy Oil, Heavy Oil (<17.5).
(2) Oil in water depth of more than 500m.
(3) Oil from oil-shales, coal, Gas-to-Liquids plants.
(4) Liquids from Natural Gas plants & gasfields.
Base Case Scenario assumes flat regular production to 2010, when ME Gulf can no longer in practice offset natural decline elsewhere ME. Gulf is Abu Dhabi, Iran, Iraq, Kuwait, NZ and Saudi Arabia, with 37% of world supply by 2010.
Venezuela I = ordinary heavy.
Venezuela II = 4 extra-heavy oil projects.

BIBLIOGRAPHY

Adelman M.A. & M.C. Lynch, 1997, 'Fixed view of resource limits creates undue pessimism', *Oil & Gas Journal*, 7 April 1997.

Ahlbrandt T., 2000, *USGS World Petroleum Assessment 2000*, USGS.

Bakhtiari A M S.,F. Shahbudaghlou, 'IEA, OPEC oil supply forecasts challenged', *Oil & Gas Journal*, 30 April 2001.

Bentley, R W., 'Global oil & gas depletion: An overview', *Energy Policy*, 30, 2002, pp. 189–205.

Campbell C.J., *The Coming Oil Crisis*, Multi-Science Publishing Co. & Petroconsultants, 1997.

Campbell C.J., and J.H. Laherrère, 'The end of cheap oil', *Scientific American*, March 1998, pp. 80–6.

Campbell C.J., F. Liesenborghs, J. Schindler, & W. Zittel, *Oelwechsel*, Deutscher Taschenbuch, 2002, ISBN 3-423-24321-4.

Campbell C.J., 'Petroleum and people'; *Population and Environment*, 24/3 November 2002.

Campbell C.J., *The Essence of Oil & Gas Depletion*; Multi-Science, 2003.

Campbell C.J., 2003, 'Industry urged to watch for regular oil production peaks, depletion signals', *Oil & Gas Journal*, 14 July 2003.

Daly H., 'Steady-state economics', *The Social Contract*, v8, 2003.

Deffeyes K.S., *Hubbert's peak – the impending world oil shortage*, Princeton University Press, 2001.

Fleay B., *The decline in the age of oil*, Pluto Press, 1995.

Fleay B., & J.H. Laherrère, 1997, 'Sustainable energy policy for Australia; submission to the Department of Primary Industry and Energy Green Paper 1996', Paper 1/97 Institute for Science and Technology Policy, Murdoch University, W. Australia.

Fleming D., 'The Next Oil Shock ?', *Prospect*, April, 1999, pp. 12–15.

Hamilton-Bergin S., 'No 19 Bus: The truth about the war and oil – the coming global energy crisis', www.no19bus.org.uk, Earthsure Foundation, UK, 2003.

Heinberg R., *The Party's Over*, New Society Publishers, 2003.

Hubbert M.K., 'Technique of prediction as applied to the production of oil & gas', in NBS Special Publication 631, US Dept. Commerce/National Bureau of Standards, 1982, pp. 16–141.

International Energy Agency, *World Energy Outlook*, 1998 edition.

Ivanhoe L.F., & Leckie G.G., 'Global oil, gas fields, sizes tallied, analyzed', *Oil & Gas Journal*, 15 Feb. 1993, pp. 87–91.

Klare M.T., *Resource wars: the new landscape of global conflict*, Owl Books, 2002.

Laherrère J.H., 1999, 'World oil supply – what goes up must come down – but when will it peak?', *Oil & Gas Journal*, 1 Feb. 1999, pp. 57–64.

Laherrère J.H., 'Is FSU oil growth sustainable?', *Petroleum Review*, April, 2002.

Laherrère J.H., Future of oil supplies; Energy Exploration & Exploitation, 2003, 21/3.

Leonard R.C., *Russian Oil And Gas: A Realistic Assessment*, Ray Leonard VP Exploration and News Ventures, YUKOS Exploration and Production, Uppsala, Sweden, May, 2002.

Longwell H., 2002, 'The future of the oil and gas industry: past approaches, new challenges', *World Energy*, 5/3, 2002.

Madron R & J. Jopling, 2003, *Gaian democracies*; Schumacher Briefings, Green Books.

Perrodon A., J.H. Laherrère and C.J. Campbell, *The world's non-conventional oil and gas*, Pet. Economist report, 1998.

Perrodon A., *Quel pétrole demain*, Technip, Paris, 1999.

Rechsteiner R., *Grun gewinnt: die letzte Olkrise und danach*, Orell Fussli, 2003.

Salameh M.G., 'Filling the global energy gap in the 21st Century', *Pet. Review*, Aug. 2002.

Scheer H., *The solar economy*, Earthscan Publications, 2002.

Simmons, M R., *Energy in the New Economy: The Limits to Growth*, Energy Institute of the Americas, October 2, 2000

Skrebowski C., 2000, 'The North Sea – a province heading for decline?', *Pet. Review*, Sept. 2002.

Smith M.R., 'Energy security in Europe', *Pet. Review*, Aug. 2002.

Society of Danish Engineers, *Oil-based technology and economy: Prospects for the Future*, 2003.

Udall S L., *The energy balloon*, McGraw Hill, 1974.

Warman H.R., 'The future of oil', *Geographical Journal*, 138/3, 1972, pp. 287–97.

Warman H.R., 'The future availability of oil', proc. conf. World Energy Supplies, by *Financial Times*, London, 1973.

Yergin D., *The Prize: the epic quest for oil, money and power*, Simon & Schuster, New York, 1991.

Youngquist W., *Geodestinies: the inevitable control of earth resources over nations and individuals*, Nat. Book Co., Portland, 1997.

Zittel W. & Schindler J., 2001, *Natural Gas – Assessment of the Term Supply Situation in Europe*, L-B-Systemtechnik Gmbh, 28 May 28 2001.

REFERENCE BOOKS

Barry R.A., 1993, *The management of international oil operations*, PennWell Books, Tulsa.

Campbell C.J., *The golden century of oil 1950–2050: the depletion of a resource*, Kluwer Academic Publishers, Dordrecht, Netherlands, 1991.

Campbell C.J., and J.H. Laherrère, 'The end of cheap oil', *Scientific American*, March 1998, pp. 80–6.

Campbell C.J., *The Coming Oil Crisis*, Multi-Science Publishing Co. & Petroconsultants, 1997.

Campbell C.J., F. Liesenborghs, J. Schindler, & W. Zittel, *Oelwechsel,* Deutscher Taschenbuch, 2002.

Campbell C.J., *The Essence of Oil & Gas Depletion*; Multi-Science, 2003.

Deffeyes K.S., *Hubbert's peak – the impending world oil shortage*; Princeton University Press, 2001.

Dowthwaite R., *The ecology of money*, Green books, 1999.

Fleay B., *The decline in the age of oil*, Pluto Press, 1995.

Fromkin D., *A peace to end all peace*, Avon Books, 1989.

Georgescu-Roegen N., *La decroissance*, Sang de Terre, Paris, 1995.

Heinberg R., *The Party's Over*, New Society Publishers, 2003.

International Energy Agency, *World Energy Outlook*, 1998.

International Energy Agency, *World Energy Outlook and impact of Economic turmoil in Asia on oil prospects*; June 1998.

International Energy Agency, *World Energy Outlook,* 1999.

International Energy Agency, *World Energy Outlook,* 2001.

Ion D.C., *The availability of world energy resources,* Graham & Trotman, 1980.

Klare M.T., , *Resource wars : the new landscape of global conflict*, Owl Books. 2002.

Madron R & J. Jopling, *Gaian democracies*, Schumacher Briefings, Green Books, 2003.

Meadows D.H. et. al, *The limits to growth*; Potomac, 1972.

Perrodon A., J.H. Laherrere and C.J. Campbell, 'The world's non-conventional oil and gas', *Pet. Economist*, 1998.

Perrodon A., *Quel pétrole demain*, Technip, Paris, 1999.

Rechsteiner R, *Grun gewinnt: die letzte Olkrise und danach*, Orell Fussli, 2003.

Sampson A. , *The seven sisters: the great oil companies and the world they created*, Coronet, London, 1988.

Scheer H., *The solar economy*; Earthscan Publications, 2002.

Schweizer P., 'Victory: the Reagan administration's secret strategy that hastened the collapse of the Soviet Union', *Atlantic Monthly Press*, New York, 1994.

Tugendhat C and A. Hamilton, *Oil – the biggest business*, Eyre Methuen, 1968.

Udall, S L., *The energy balloon*; 1974, McGraw Hill.

Udall, S L., *The Myths of August*, Rutgers University Press, 1998.

Yergin D., *The Prize: the epic quest for oil, money and power,* Simon & Schuster, New York, 1991.

Youngquist W., 1997, *Geodestinies: the inevitable control of earth resources over nations and individuals*; Nat. Book Co., Portland, 1997.

Notes

Notes